Treat Yourself Right!

Treat Yourself Right!

Torah Guidelines for
Maintaining Your Health and Safety

TARGUM/FELDHEIM

First published 2001
Copyright © 2001 by M. Goldberger
ISBN 1-56871-280-4

Published by:
Targum Press, Inc.
22700 W. Eleven Mile Rd.
Southfield, MI 48034
E-mail: targum@netvision.net.il
Fax toll-free: 888-298-9992

Distributed by:
Feldheim Publishers
200 Airport Executive Park
Nanuet, NY 10954
www.feldheim.com

Printed in Israel

With special thanks to

Rabbi Eliezer Gevirtz
Rabbi Menachem Goldman
Mordechai Gelber
Yitzchak E. Gold
B. Siegel
Charlie Mamiye
and others.

A special thank you to Rabbi and Mrs. Eliezer Hamburger, directors of the Torah Safety Commission, for their valuable assistance.

In memory of
Yosef ben Arline
ת.נ.צ.ב.ה.

In loving memory of our dear brother,
brother-in-law, and uncle

Yosef ben Arline

David and Valerie Mizrahi
and family

May this book serve as a memorial to

Maran HaRav Avigdor Miller, zt"l,

*who suggested that
we write on this topic.*

Contents

Preface

Guard your souls exceedingly.

(*Devarim* 4:15)

We are taught in *Bereishis* (1:26) that Hashem created man in His image. This fundamental principle teaches us the greatness of people and their responsibilities to themselves and to each other. We are taught that "he who sheds the blood of a person is liable because Hashem created man in His image" (*Bereishis* 9:6). If a person is aware of his intrinsic value as a human being, he will do his utmost to care for his own health and safety.

A person is obligated to protect his own life, the gift he was given by Hashem, as well as protect the lives of others. Many of us go through our lives without giving much thought to safety and health hazards that surround us. This can lead to serious danger, *chas v'shalom*. We must recognize our greatness as people created in the image of Hashem and our responsibility to ourselves.

> *Always be on guard for yourself and guard your soul exceedingly.*

(Ibid. 4:9)

The commandment to take care of our bodies is unique in that it urges us to guard ourselves not only from danger but even from the possibility of danger. Our lives are precious. One moment of life in this world is worth more than all of life in the next world (*Avos* 4:17). Every moment of life holds the potential for Torah learning and performing good deeds, which give us priceless rewards in *Olam HaBa* (*Peleh Yoeitz, Shemirah*).

The Creator instructs us to "choose life" (*Devarim* 30:19), not death. Another *pasuk* teaches, "You shall live by them [the *mitzvos*]" (*Vayikra* 18:5). We are in this world to accomplish, and we need to be healthy in order to function well.

When the Torah describes Yaakov's return to Eretz Yisrael, it states: "He came complete" (*Bereishis* 33:18). The Talmud (*Shabbos* 33b) explains that it refers to three dimensions: his health, his finances, and his Torah studies. These are the dimensions of completion for every person's body and *neshamah*.

I have given the Levi'im as a gift to Aharon and to
his sons from among the children of Israel, to do the
service of the children of Israel in the Ohel Moed
and to atone for the children of Israel, so that there
will be no plague among the children of Israel when
the children of Israel approach the Sanctuary.

(Bemidbar 8:19)

Rashi points out that the phrase "the children of Israel," b'nei Yisrael, is repeated five times in this verse, like the five books of the Torah, demonstrating Hashem's great love for us. Why was this particular verse selected to convey this message?

Rav Avigdor Miller, zt"l, in his book *Journey into Greatness* (pp. 94–95) explains that this verse highlights the extreme importance of ensuring the safety of the Jewish nation. Protecting the lives of the holy people is a primary consideration of the Torah.

With this in mind, let us learn more about what the Torah says regarding taking care of our bodies and ensuring our good health and safety.

Chapter One

Logical Laws

Hashem created people with built-in wisdom, an intuition which helps us determine what is right and wrong. Thus, a person is bound to obey his common sense as if it gives him direct commands from Hashem.

When the Sages were searching for a verse to prove a certain point, an objection would often be raised: "Why do you need a verse for this? It can be derived through logic!" (*Bava Kama* 46b). We see clearly that logic is equivalent to a verse in the Torah.

Even before the Torah was given Hashem held wrongdoers accountable for their deeds and punished them. The generation of Noach and the people of Sedom and Amorah are two examples of this. Why were they considered responsible for their deeds? Rav Nissim Gaon (in his preface to *Maseches*

Berachos) explains: "All mitzvos that can be understood by one's logic and common sense were obligatory upon people from the beginning of Creation, for all generations."

Caring for our bodes and ensuring the safety of our lives and others is a prime example of a logic mitzvah. "One may not cause any other person or oneself to die, even unintentionally. All the safety traffic laws for drivers and pedestrians are included [in this rule]" (Rav Avigdor Miller, *A Nation Is Born*, p. 281).

Rav Chatzkel Levenstein, *zt"l*, used to say that most traffic accidents are caused by wild, reckless driving. When we drive, we are obligated to obey traffic rules, observe speed limits, and do our utmost to ensure the safety of ourselves, our passengers, and other drivers.

It is also extremely important to take proper precautions against fire, which can rage out of control and threaten lives. Parents must protect their children from burning candles, fires on stoves, and barbecues.

A home has many potential hazards for young children, including electrical outlets and open windows. We have a responsibility to make our homes as safe as possible, for children and adults alike. The

Torah instructs us to build a guard rail around a roof: "When you build [or buy or rent] a new house, you must make a [sturdy] fence [at least ten handbreadths high]. Do not be one who sheds blood by allowing [the potential for] someone to fall off your roof" (*Devarim* 22:8). One may not endanger others by ignoring proper health and safety guidelines.

> *He who desires to be devoted to Hashem, let him fulfill the laws of preventing damages.*
>
> (*Bava Kama* 30a)

We must learn to value life as the Torah does, to cherish and prolong one's life as much as possible and to protect our well-being and health with the fervor that is due every mitzvah.

> *If an ox gores a man or a woman to death, the ox shall be stoned to death....*
>
> (*Shemos* 21:28)

"Even if the goring was unexpected, some blame is placed on the owner. A crime of even minor negligence that caused a loss of someone's life is extremely severe. We kill the ox as a symbol of the killing of the owner" (*A Nation Is Born*, p. 306).

If the owner had been warned but he did not watch his animal, the ox is stoned and Hashem shall put the owner to death as well (*Shemos* 21:29).

Negligence that causes a death is punishable by Hashem's laws. This applies to negligence regarding a wild ox, a rickety ladder, an open window, a loose railing, or carelessness with fire. When the harm was indirect, *beis din* does not punish, but the Heavenly *beis din* considers the person guilty to some degree.

A person should never place himself in a dangerous situation for he may not be saved by a miracle. If he is saved, it will be deducted from his merits.

(*Shabbos* 32a)

If an individual was negligent with his life, Hashem may perform a miracle on his behalf, but this is contrary to Hashem's preferred way of running this world. Hence, the recipient is debited for the miracle. "A person is held less in esteem by Hashem if He changes the laws of nature for the person [i.e., a miracle is performed for him] than if he is helped through natural means" (ibid. 53b).

Thus we are always obligated to guard our health and life (see *Devarim* 4:9, 15 and *Berachos* 32b). Preventing harm to our own bodies is as important as preventing harm to any other Jew's body.

Chapter Two

Lack of Caution

I shall provide a place for him to flee to.

(Shemos 21:13)

One who unintentionally killed someone through negligence or carelessness has to flee to a city of refuge to gain atonement. We see from this that a person's lack of sufficient caution is considered a crime. One who causes harm or loss to others because he neglects to use foresight and discretion is guilty by Hashem's standards.

The cities of refuge were communities inhabited by the Levi'im, who were Torah teachers (*Devarim* 33:10). One who killed unintentionally was confined there so that he would learn from the Levi'im the severity of his lack of sufficient caution. A person is held responsible if he keeps a vicious animal or a rickety ladder on his property, leaves windows open without window guards, or allows other potential dangers.

We are admonished by the Torah to care for our health and be concerned for safety. Verses 4:9 and

4:15 in *Devarim* teach this in terms of guarding one's soul, but the Gemara explains that it refers also to physical safety (*Berachos* 32b).

> *Who is wise? He who sees the future.*
>
> (*Tamid* 32a)

There are several principles which must be recalled when learning proper safety guidelines the Torah way:

❖ Hashem loves every individual always. He never changes His feelings for people. If a person sins, Hashem desires that person's repentance. A sin is a tragedy, a fearful catastrophe that casts darkness upon the person's soul and upon the entire universe. Hashem prefers that we never sin, but if we do stumble, He looks forward to our repentance (as we say in the blessing for repentance in *Shemoneh Esrei*).

❖ It is difficult to be happy and to serve Hashem properly when one is ill. One is therefore obligated to take care of his health and maintain it as much as possible.

❖ Everyone dies eventually. We have to be circumspect to maintain and promote our health and well-being, but, at the same time, not to become nervous wrecks over it. Our health is a most precious commodity that Hashem provides and maintains for a certain number of years, but not forever. Make the most of your life on earth.

❖ Life comes with a guarantee from Hashem that we will not suffer if we follow the Torah's laws. The Rambam (*Hilchos Dei'os* 4:20) words it in this manner:

Every person who maintains these practices [to care for his health according to Torah guidelines] is guaranteed not to be ill during his lifetime, until he becomes very old. He shall not need a physician and he will be healthy all his days, unless he was born with a defect, he conducted himself improperly, or there is an epidemic or famine.

This teaches us that if we follow the Torah's guidelines for health and safety, Hashem will help us succeed. As we learn in *Shemos* (15:26): "If you listen to the voice of Hashem, your God, and you do what is right in His eyes, and you obey His commandments, every sickness that I placed on Egypt I will not place upon you, for I am Hashem your Healer." (See *Tur, Orach Chaim* 116.)

Fear of Hashem increases one's days, but the years of the wicked will be shortened.

(*Mishlei* 10:27)

Chapter Three

Heart and Mouth Safety

[The Torah and mitzvos] are your life; they lengthen your days.

(*Devarim* 30:20)

Studies have established that there is a lesser incidence of heart attacks among Torah-observant Jews than there is among the general population. *The International Journal of Cardiology* explains this phenomenon: "It is possible that the strong belief in a Supreme Being and the role of prayer may in themselves be protective" (January, 1986).

A Jew's faith in Hashem reduces the stress and anxiety that come along with living in an extremely complex society, thus decreasing the incidence of stress-related heart ailments. This is a clear example of how a long, healthy life can be a fringe benefit of a person's faith in Hashem.

We are taught in the Talmud that we should not

converse while eating or drinking so as not to endanger our lives (*Taanis* 5b). It's interesting to note that there have been a number of famous and infamous people throughout history, up to the present day, who have choked to death while eating.

The wind pipes and food pipes, abutting each other, each possess their own vital functions. Statistics show that one-sixth of all fatal accidents in the home are caused by food becoming lodged in the windpipe as a result of speaking while eating. Hence, the Gemara and the *Shulchan Aruch* (*Orach Chaim* 170:1) teach us to avoid these dangers. The *Shulchan Aruch* (ibid.) adds, "Even if someone happens to sneeze during a meal, do not say to him 'to your health' while you are eating." The *Mishnah Berurah* adds that one should not even speak words of Torah with food in his mouth. *Divrei Torah* should only be said between courses.

There are many obvious safety precautions that are related to these teachings. Some examples are:

❖ Make sure not to leave small objects, such as toy parts, balloons, rubber bands, pins, and beads, within a baby's reach. He can easily put these things into his mouth and choke or swallow them.

❖ Keep certain foods away from young children.

Taffy, nuts, raisins, popcorn, and sucking candies can easily be choked on.

❖ Beware of small rattles, which have been known to cause choking deaths.

❖ Insist that your children sit while eating, and never run, walk, or play with food in their mouths. This is especially important with hard candy and lollipops.

❖ Be sure to cut food into small pieces for younger children, and supervise the food that older children give younger children.

It would be commendable to learn the Heimlich Maneuver, which has been publicized as a means of dislodging food caught in the windpipe. However, this technique serves as a possible remedy if one is in trouble, whereas not talking while chewing food is a preventative to avoid danger in the first place. We must be sure to learn, obey, and teach this important, life-preserving halachah.

Chapter Four

The King's Statue

One should wash his face daily in honor of the Creator.

(*Shabbos* 50b)

The Midrash compares this concept to a statue of the king which is placed in every town square throughout the kingdom (*Vayikra Rabbah* 32:3). How the townspeople care for the statue indicates to the king how they care about him. Hillel explains that this is why bathing, eating, and caring for our bodies are great mitzvos. When we care for our bodies, having in mind that we were created in Hashem's image and we reflect Hashem's unlimited greatness, we are testifying to the greatness of the Creator.

Sometimes we see people willing to undergo certain discomforts for their physical pleasure, even when this is harmful to their bodies. Smoking is one example of this. There are people who choose to leave their comfortable work environments to smoke outside, since they're not allowed to smoke inside the building. It is a pitiful sight to see them sweating away in the heat of the summer or huddled against the building in the freezing winter, puffing away, unwilling to control their urge to smoke.

Just as these people understand the need to be concerned for others' health, they should be concerned for their own health. We are obligated to care for our bodies and prevent harm from befalling them. A person who neglects to care for his own health by smoking is indicating his lack of respect for his Creator (or his ignorance of the issues involved).

On the other hand, when we care for a Jew's welfare, we are rewarded.

"Charity rescues from death" (*Mishlei* 10:2). In some cases, giving charity can redeem one from a death penalty decreed by Heaven (*Rosh HaShanah* 16b).

When we give charity, we are demonstrating that we desire to help other people live. This is a great mitzvah and a form of repentance, since we show that we care for the lives and safety of our brethren. Thus we are rewarded, measure for measure, with having our own lives rescued.

Chapter Five

Dogs and Ladders

The title of this chapter, similar to the name of a popular board game, should help you remember the Gemara in *Bava Kama* (15b) that teaches: "From where do we know that one may not raise a wild dog in his home or keep a shaky ladder around? From the verse: 'Do not put blood in your home' (*Devarim* 22:8)." This teaching is quoted in the name of Rabbi Nassan three times in Shas, each time with the same two examples: dogs and ladders.

The Maharsha explains that although these items can be controlled, it is nonetheless forbidden to maintain a potential hazard in one's home. One of the members of the household may forget about the danger, or a visitor who is not aware of the danger may be injured. Furthermore, the Maharsha adds, one may not justify owning an attack dog because he wants the added security or protection from potential thieves.

These lessons can be applied in many ways. For example, one who uses a weak ladder or another unsteady support to reach a high shelf or to hang up curtains is risking the potential of "putting blood in his home," *chas v'shalom.*

In addition, one needs to keep his home free of the clutter of children's toys in places where people may trip and fall, and make sure that all knives, matches, medicine, and household chemicals are out of a child's reach. Burning candles are especially dangerous, even if they are for Shabbos, *yom tov,* Chanukah, or a *yahrtzeit.* They can never be left near unsupervised children. Leaving a window open without a screen is similar to having a porch without a guard railing.

As the Gemara teaches us, a wise person is one who anticipates and protects himself from problems (*Tamid* 32a).

The Gemara speaks further on the subject of a wild dog:

> One who raises a wild dog in his home prevents chesed from being performed in his house...and removes fear of Heaven from himself.
>
> (Shabbos 63a–b)

Why should this be so? Rashi explains that poor

people will be afraid to come to the home for help because of the dog. This will inevitably result in a decrease in the amount of *chesed* performed there.

The Maharsha notes that when a person thinks that his dog will protect him, he is no longer focusing on his mezuzah, which teaches us to fear Hashem. Even if the owner knows that the dog will not actually hurt anyone, a potential burglar does not know this, and the owner will come to trust in his dog and not in Hashem.

This does not mean that one should not invest in an alarm system or leave his doors unlocked. We are required to invest in the necessary efforts, while at the same time keeping in mind that it is Hashem Who is keeping us safe. Inappropriate or insufficient efforts to protect oneself are deemed transgression and not *hishtadlus*.

Chapter Six

Breathing Bonus

Our bodies are the vehicles that enable us to live and serve Hashem. Therefore, keeping your body energized will enrich your life by allowing you to perform every mitzvah with vitality.

There are many things we should be doing to maintain our good health for long-term service to Hashem. It is essential, though, to keep what we do simple and practical so that we follow through with these practices regularly.

One example of a simple, practical behavior which will improve our sense of well-being is breathing properly. "For every breath we take, we ought to praise Hashem" (*Bereishis Rabbah* 14:11).

If you train yourself to take one slow, deep, strainless breath every hour, with the intention of relaxing, you will find yourself energized and uplifted. Begin by taking a nice deep breath right now and exhaling slowly with the thought, *Baruch Hashem, I am able to breathe with ease!*

Some of the benefits of breathing deeply include:

- ❖ More focus
- ❖ More alertness
- ❖ Strength
- ❖ Relaxation
- ❖ Thoughts of gratitude to Hashem
- ❖ More motivation and joy

Hashem continually provides us with abundant air to breathe. Let us attempt to train ourselves to appreciate this gift on an ongoing basis.

Imagine if there were air meters on every corner. How much would we pay to indulge in a breath of Hashem's miracle air?

In general, the more we simplify our lives and train ourselves to be responsive to pleasures that are always readily accessible, the more we benefit. Life becomes more exciting when you learn how to enjoy the simple act of breathing Hashem's air. Tune yourself in to Hashem's bounty and recognize the joys in seeing with your eyes, hearing with your ears, feeling with your fingers, and thinking with your brain.

Chapter Seven

Skin Care

Our skin serves many functions for which we have to thank Hashem.

Each square inch of skin contains approximately four million cells, five yards of nerves, four feet of blood vessels, one hundred and twenty sweat glands, twenty oil glands, and thirty nerve endings.

The skin is truly a marvelous contrivance designed, created, and maintained by the Creator, yet we tend to neglect to appreciate it.

The skin is the frontier of the body. It serves as a shield to protect the body from the environment, like a suit of armor. It manufactures vitamin D when exposed to sunlight, assists in regulating the body's blood pressure, and serves to waterproof the body. It keeps water out of the body when one is immersed in a tub or a pool, and it keeps water in so that a person does not dehydrate.

The skin also contains a complex nervous system. All throughout our skin there are nerve endings which perceive pain, heat, and cold, and also provide the sense of touch. The skin houses a wide array of receptors and detectors which inform us about the world through sensations such as heat, cold, pressure, pain, or contact. The skin is not merely a cover for our body; it is an organ that serves many functions.

The invasion of bacteria is arrested by the skin, unless there is a break in its surface.

When a break does occur in the skin, it has the remarkable ability to regenerate and actually reunite itself. We must appreciate the incredible phenomenon of such a miracle! Imagine a garment which, if it tears, would mend itself within a week or two. How much would such a garment be worth?

The skin renews itself on a regular basis. In about a month, a human being grows an entirely new outer skin, although this is not noticeable because it develops gradually.

The skin serves as an insulator to conserve body heat. It also provides "air conditioning," consisting of about two million sweat glands all over the body and about six miles of ducts. With this system, the body manufactures sweat, which evaporates from the surface of the skin, cooling the body.

The skin serves as a shock absorber. Areas that receive the most wear have extra protection in the form of calluses. Different parts of the body have different types of skin, tougher or softer, and differing amounts of hair (which the skin also produces), based on the need of protection in that specific area. The skin is also remarkably elastic in order to allow for many different body positions and limb flexing.

There are so many miraculous benefits in this marvelous creation that covers the entire body. The average person has about eighteen square feet of skin which fit around him perfectly.

Unfortunately, statistics show that approximately one million Americans are developing different forms of skin cancer and seventeen thousand lives are lost from this disease annually. The numbers are only increasing. Why is this happening? Scientists attribute it to a prevalent increase in leisure time. People with nothing to do sit in the sun for long hours and develop skin disease.

This points to a great and fundamental lesson — to be sure to utilize our body and skin for worthwhile endeavors. Chazal admonish us in *Pirkei Avos* (1:10) to "love work" — to avoid idleness, and to always keep busy. The Gemara teaches that idleness leads to mental instability and immorality (*Kesubos* 39b). It is a person's obligation to see to it that he uses his skin properly, to sweat for Torah and mitzvos, and not to abuse it by sitting lazily in the sun.

When we study the list of recommendations for preventing skin cancer, we are inspired to be more careful with the laws of modesty. The experts says that exposure to the sun's rays should be limited. When outdoors, one should cover as much skin as possible by wearing a long-sleeved shirt and a hat that shades the face, neck, and ears. Children in particular should be protected from the sun.

In truth, being modest in dress and actions protects and accentuates the greatness of a Jew. When we cover our body, we demonstrate that the primary uniqueness of a person is within, the soul that fills the body. Protection from skin cancer is only a side benefit. However, in every generation there are new diseases that Hashem sends to punish for new *aveiros* (sins), measure for measure. Since many people in today's world are overstepping the bounds of decency by not dressing properly, perhaps Hashem is punishing them, measure for measure, with this horrific disease.

Rather than dwelling on the negative, let us remember that by properly caring for our skin, we will be able to serve Hashem in the most energetic way.

Chapter Eight

Feet Care

*The footsteps of a person are established by
Hashem, and his way is desired. Even if he falls, he
is not forsaken, for Hashem is supporting his hand.*

(Tehillim 37:23–24)

The Gemara teaches that if a person stubs his toe
he should realize that it was by Heavenly decree
(*Chullin* 7b). The above verses are quoted as proof to
this. We learn that our feet themselves are a gift of
support, provided by Hashem, and if we get a bruise
there is a message in that, too.

How do we begin to deal with this far reaching
subject? Let us begin with prayer.

*A person should always pray that he will continue to
be healthy in his old age. His eyes should function,
his mouth should be able to eat, his feet should be
able to walk....*

(Midrash Tanchuma, Mikeitz 10)

We can say this prayer every day, beginning right now. When one happens to see an older person suffering from infirmities, it is good to recall this prayer. The more you say it, the more you will benefit from it.

The *Mishnah* in *Ohalos* (1:8) will help us appreciate all the components of our feet. We are taught that "there are 248 bones in a person's body: thirty in the foot (six in each toe), ten at the ankle, two at the calf, five at the knee, one at the thigh, three at the top of the thigh. Thus there are fifty-one bones in each leg, a total of 102 for the two feet."

Consider the many miraculous wonders of your feet:

They keep you standing in perfect balance. A table or chair cannot stand on two feet, but you can!

You can even balance on one foot for short periods of time when necessary.

The two feet keep growing at the same rate from birth so that you are always in balance. We have to appreciate the fact that they are symmetrical at birth, and that they continue to develop at the exact same rate (Rabbi Avigdor Miller, *Rejoice O Youth*, p. 99).

Walking is a delight for a thinking person. The bones flex in effortless motion, with smoothly functioning joints bathed in antifriction liquid. The knee and other bones bend and straighten without any sensation of chafing, scraping, or creaking. The ankle joints and complex arch bones flex and relax in an easy motion. We must thank Hashem daily, with heartfelt gratitude, for guiding our steps!

There are dozens of muscles in the legs for movement, and hundreds of ligaments that hold the bones together. The weight-bearing parts of the foot have the thickest skin of the body. There is fat and fibrous connective tissue in the sole of the foot to provide cushioning and shock absorption.

In a sense, Hashem has designed our feet as miracle shoes with all the comforts of a deluxe, lifetime-guaranteed model.

How important is it for a person to take care of his feet? How much money should he spend toward this effort? The Gemara (*Shabbos* 129a) states emphatically: "A person should even sell the beams of his house in order to buy shoes for his feet"! Another version of this *gemara* says that a person should even sell all that he owns in order to buy shoes.

It is important to thank Hashem for the ability to walk. We all know how to do it. Once we learn as children we usually maintain the skill for the duration of our lives. One good way to maintain your overall physical fitness is to take daily walks. There are many advantages to this form of exercise:

❖ You don't need special equipment. (A good pair of shoes is helpful.)

❖ It's easy to fit into your schedule.

❖ You can walk anywhere.

❖ It can be done indoors in inclement weather.

❖ It helps control one's weight.

❖ It is beneficial for the body's cardiovascular system. (It's interesting to note that the current view of many exercise experts is that brisk walking is an even better and safer form of cardiovascular exercise than jogging or running, since it does not involve the potential of impact-related injuries to the joints and back.)

These are some of the reasons that Chazal may have considered walking as one of the three essentials in a body-fitness program.

The Gemara teaches:

Be careful in three matters: Do not sit too much, for that may lead to certain ailments. Do not stand excessively, for that is harmful to the heart. Do not walk too much, for that is detrimental to the eyesight. Rather, spend one-third of your time sitting, one-third of your time standing, and one-third of your time walking.

(*Kesubos* 111a)

Just as it is obvious to us that sitting is beneficial, since it allows the heart and the rest of the body to rest, it is essential for us to also stand and walk for exercise. Hashem designed us with these functions in mind, and we are obligated to maintain a healthy balance of these activities.

In order to maintain a regular walking schedule, it is important to make it a fun activity. Some suggestions are:

1. "Walking with the wise will make you wise" (Mishlei 13:20). Choose a walking partner. Your walking time will pass in a more enjoyable way, and you will be more motivated to stick with it. It can also be a good way of spending quality time with a teacher, parent, spouse, sibling, or child.

2. Listen to a Torah tape on a Walkman as you go. Your mind and body will be reenergized at the same time. (Please write us at Box 82, Staten Island, NY 10309, for a free tape sample.)

It is important to remember the following safety guidelines when walking: Wear reflective clothing at night so that drivers can see you, cross at crosswalks and only when the light is green, look both ways before you cross, keep your eye out for turning cars, and never stand in the street while waiting for the light to change. These may seem like simple rules, but how often do we ignore them in our hurry to get somewhere? If we're walking for our health, let us remember how important safety is.

Chapter Nine

Bone Care

Let us now analyze some of the benefits we gain from our bones and their many functions:

Bones form the skeleton which is the frame of the body. Without them we would collapse like a blob of jelly. We would not be able to walk, talk, sit, or move. The bone frame actually holds up a mass of muscles and organs that may weigh five times more than the bones themselves.

The bones contain the body's mineral supply. They are warehouses of calcium and phosphorus that operate twenty-four hours a day.

The bones are factories. The skeletal system not only provides support for the body, but it also contributes to the blood supply through bone marrow. The marrow manufactures millions of red blood cells that enable us to breathe, as well as a lesser amount of white blood cells which protect us from infection by battling against all types of invading germs. The bone marrow manufactures about ten billion defender cells daily to keep you fit and healthy!

The bones are exceptionally strong in order to protect the vulnerable parts of the body. The eyes, for example, are surrounded by a bone casing to protect them from injury, as are many other soft organs and tissues. We have to thank Hashem for each bone of the body (a total of 248 times) and for their multiple functions.

In addition to thanking Hashem for providing us with bones that protect many parts of the body, we should remember the following verse (which is part of the Shabbos prayers):

> Hashem protects all of [a righteous person's] bones, not even one of them has been broken!
>
> (Tehillim 34:21)

Bones bear the weight of the body. Different bones have different strengths based on where they are situated and how great a part they play in weight bearing. The spinal column is light and porous so that it can accomplish its functions. Other bones are dense and super-strong. Some bones are stronger than a solid block of steel of the same size, and the thigh bone is usually stronger, pound for pound, than reinforced concrete!

Bones become stronger as they are needed. Babies' bones are soft and flexible so that they can pass through the birth canal. They maintain a certain softness throughout childhood to allow for growth and to guard against damage in scrapes and falls, but they harden toward adulthood.

If a bone breaks, it can regenerate. A physician may put the bone back in place and immobilize it in a cast to maintain the proper position. The healing itself, however, comes from the bone, which begins to produce overtime to replace that which is lacking. The torn blood capillaries form a clot. Cells called "macrophages" invade the clot and devour the debris. Bone cells begin to multiply and produce new bone tissue. There are even "cell repairmen" within bones which serve to destroy the jagged edges of the break so that the bone will heal properly! A ring of new bone tissue is formed around the fracture to reinforce the mended bone. The bone engages in a process called "remodeling" so that eventually it appears as if the bone has never been broken.

If you have ever broken a bone in your lifetime, you must thank Hashem for repairing it like new and for the other 247 bones that have not been broken.

As we study the messages of our bones, we can reach a new and dynamic understanding of the connection between the 248 bones of the body and the 248 positive commandments of the Torah. The verse in *Tehillim* teaches us, "Hashem protects all of [a righteous person's] bones, not even one of them has been broken" (34:21). Because the tzaddik observes the mitzvos, which correspond to the number of bones in his body, he is assured of strong and healthy bones.

Just as bones uphold and strengthen the body, preventing its collapse, Hashem has provided us with mitzvos which uphold our spiritual essence. Without them, man would disintegrate and cease to exist. Even if only one bone is broken, a person may be crippled or suffer extensively. So too, if a person is lacking even one mitzvah, his soul is crippled. And some mitzvos are so vital that without them a person cannot exist at all.

The Gemara (*Pesachim* 56a) relates that King Chizkiyahu concealed a unique book of healing that was used for curing many ailments. The Sages approved of his action, Rashi explains, because people were relying on the book to achieve immediate cures instead of humbling themselves in repentance and praying for mercy to become well.

Pain and suffering serve as rebukes to a person. They are messages from Hashem which cannot be ignored. When a person is suffering in some way, he is instructed to search for the measure-for-measure reason for which he is being punished (*Berachos* 5b).

If we find ourselves suffering from some kind of ailment, we should consult both a physician — for the body — and a Torah sage — for the soul. It is uniquely appropriate that the mitzvos correspond to all the bones of the body, for a Jew is required to devote himself entirely to serving Hashem.

Chapter Ten

Teeth Care

The Gemara (*Pesachim* 113a) relates several health lessons that Rav taught his son, Rabbi Chiya:

1. "Do not accustom yourself to using medicine." The reason for this, Rashi and Rashbam explain, is to avoid developing a dependency on medication, which will be a waste of money and may result in detrimental side effects. Medicine should only be used as a last resort.

2. "Do not walk with large steps." Hurrying from place to place may diminish one's eyesight. Although we learned from the *gemara* in *Kesubos* *that one should spend one-third of his time walking, it is important to avoid taking large steps during your walking session.*

3. "Do not rush to have your teeth pulled." At times your teeth may ache, but if you are patient and clean and brush your teeth, and listen

to the advice of a competent dentist, the pain may eventually subside.

We have to appreciate and thank Hashem for our incredible teeth. Without them, it would be almost impossible to eat. The teeth are part of an amazing laboratory. They begin the body's digestive system by first cutting our food to chewing size and then grinding it down to smaller and smaller pieces. The rest of the mouth aids the teeth in doing their job — saliva is secreted to facilitate chewing and digestion and the tongue propels the pieces of food to the right positions for biting and grinding. (The sensitive tongue also darts back and forth over the food to feel out bits of bone and other indigestible matter.) The system is amazing, but we must allow it to work properly. The Gemara encourages us to eat slowly and to chew our food well in order to be healthy (*Shabbos* 152a).

Our Creator gives us teeth precisely when we need them. A newborn baby has no teeth at all. His mouth is designed for nursing so that he can derive the nourishment most suited for him — his mother's milk. At approximately six months of age, when the baby begins to need other foods, his teeth start to grow out of his gums.

Later, as a child's jaw begins to grow to adult

size, his baby teeth fall out in order to allow for larger teeth to grow in. However, only a few teeth fall out at a time, so that the child can continue to chew food in the interim! (*Chovos HaLevovos, bechinah 5*).

Teeth serve as the framework for the mouth. If not for teeth, the mouth would collapse, as is evident by the appearance of people who have become edentulous.

Teeth also assist in the speaking process. Many sounds can only be made with the help of our teeth. It is important, though, to only use the power of speech for the right words. As David HaMelech points out:

> *What do you gain and what increase will you achieve from a deceitful tongue?*

(*Tehillim* 120:3)

This verse, the Gemara explains, refers to the physical design of the tongue, which is unique among the other organs of the body in several ways:

- ❖ The other limbs are situated in upright positions. The tongue, however, is stationed in a horizontal position.
- ❖ The other limbs are outside the body, whereas the tongue is housed inside.
- ❖ The tongue is surrounded by two walls, one of

bone and one of flesh — the jaw bones and the lips. Hashem provided these special barricades in order to enclose the tongue.

Rabbi Yochanan teaches (in the name of Rabbi Yosi ben Zimra) that all this is to help us guard against improper speech (*Arachin* 15b).

The teeth serve as a lock and key for the tongue. When one is tempted to divulge a juicy piece of gossip and has to battle with himself to prevent it from slipping out, he can use this barrier of bone and flesh to clamp down. The three unique characteristics of the tongue are meant to teach us how careful we must be with this valuable piece of equipment. Treat your teeth properly, by brushing them and cleaning them regularly, so that they can assist you in time of need — namely to guard against *lashon hara*!

Chapter Eleven

Brain and Mind Care

Of all the good things that one must guard, he must guard his mind, because from it come all the results of life.

(Mishlei 4:23)

The brain is one of our greatest gifts from Hashem. Not only is it the most perfect computer in the universe, but it is also the computer that invented all other computers!

The brain consists of about three pounds of gray and white tissue, but it has extraordinary capacities. No computer comes near duplicating the brain's myriad functions. The human mind is estimated to be capable of storing fifteen trillion separate pieces of information, and it can simultaneously receive and transmit as many messages as one thousand large switchboards, of the type needed for a city as densely populated as New York. It contains a stag-

gering number of components: about thirty billion
nerve cells that are all interconnected — some as
many as sixty thousand times — all in the compact
area of a human skull! To perform all these functions, the brain uses about half of the body's blood
and oxygen supply.

The brain serves as a built-in alarm system for
the body. It recognizes danger signals and allows us
to react to them, either by avoiding the danger alto-
gether or minimizing its impact. It also allows us to
experience pain so that we can take proper healing
steps, and allows us to record the experience in our
memory so that we will be able to prevent similar situations in the future.

> One who has a good heart [i.e., mind] is at a con-
> stant [and everlasting] feast.
>
> (Mishlei 15:15)

One of the most important ingredients required
for a long and healthy life is a healthy mind. The
proper Torah attitudes engender this health.

Examples of these attitudes are:

1. The ability to perceive the good in all things, as
   indicated by the verse: "Hashem saw all that He
   made, and behold, it was very good!" (Bereishis
   1:31).

2. The understanding that all that transpires is good in some way, as the Gemara teaches, "All that the Merciful One does is for good" (*Berachos* 60b).

These attitudes will bring us happiness, like David HaMelech says, "You cause me happiness by Your work, I sing at the deeds of Your Hands" (*Tehillim* 92:5).

Good health and all forms of happiness will be the result of the correct attitudes toward life. The mind can be trained to constantly rejoice, under any and all circumstances. Life is filled with intense pleasures which are available to us all, if we develop the proper, Torah mental attitude.

We must learn to enjoy breathing air, drinking water, eating proper amounts of food, experiencing the sunlight, the wind, the rain, the moon, the stars, the use of our limbs, our five senses.... The list is endless!

We can develop our minds and senses to experience and enjoy life to the extent that living will be a feast. This life is the pathway to closeness to Hashem which prepares us for the World to Come.

Chapter Twelve

Avoid Anger

Those who are besieged by anger have no life.
(*Pesachim* 113b)

Avoiding anger is an important component to caring for our health. It is well known that besides ruining relationships, anger can produce physical ailments such as headaches, stomach problems, aches and pains, and depression. Even if there are no obvious physical manifestations of the anger, it may still be buried within, causing long-term physical damage.

For the sake of your own health, it is important to learn to control your anger. Tests have been done on the levels of hostility in people. Those who ranked the highest in hostility were found to have a 20-percent higher mortality rate.

Anger has especially been linked to heart disease. Angry people are more susceptible to heart attacks, which is a leading cause of death in the United States. Anger raises one's blood pressure and leads to increased clogging of the arteries. Thus, the risk of heart attack is greatly increased during the two hours following a bout with anger.

> *Hashem loves...those who do not get angry.*
> (*Pesachim* 113b)

> *Regarding those who always get angry, we can assume that their sins outnumber their merits.*
> (*Nedarim* 22b)

"One who removes anger from his system will be saved from Gehinnom and he will merit *Olam HaBa*" (*Shemiras HaLashon, Tevunah* 13). People who have survived cardiac arrest attest to this lesson. They feel that they will remain healthier if they do not quarrel anymore.

The AAA's Foundation for Traffic Safety reports on a phenomenon they call "road rage" (the highway threat of drivers who become enraged at the driving of other people and are intent on getting even), where anger escalates into battle and ends tragically. These incidents have increased by over 50 percent in five years. The National Highway Traffic Safety Administration estimates that as many as two-thirds of all fatal crashes are associated with aggressive driving behavior.

How can you avoid provoking anger in others on the road? Two suggestions are not to drive too slowly in a fast lane and not to tailgate. You can also defuse a potentially dangerous situation by making sure you do not become angry at anyone while on the road. Pull back and be very patient. Never try to teach another driver a lesson. When a person becomes enraged and loses control, he can easily cause danger to those on the road around him. You must drill yourself in advance to make sure you react appropriately to altercations.

Tell yourself, "Who is a wise person? He who foresees the consequences of his actions" (*Tamid* 32a).

Would you rather be arrogant and proud but dead, or humble and alive?

When the great Sage Rabbi Nechunya was asked, "What is the secret to your longevity?" he responded, "I was always easygoing. I never acted stubbornly" (*Megillah* 28a).

Similarly, when Rav Eliyahu Lopian (who lived to be close to one hundred) was asked for his secret, he said, "I never become angry at anyone for anything." This is very similar to the answer of the Sage Rabbi Ada bar Ahavah, who said, "In all my life I have never been upset in my home" (*Taanis* 20b).

Rava taught, "One who is easy to get along with will be forgiven for all of his sins" (*Rosh HaShanah* 17a). Rashi explains that a person who is easy to get along with is one who does not hold onto grudges. He is quick to forgive those who slight him.

Our Sages teach us to avoid actual anger even for a mitzvah, such as when necessary for teaching children or disciples. One should only pretend to be angry. (Other commentaries, such as Rabbeinu Yonah on *Avos*, teach that there are rare times when it is appropriate for a person to actually become angry.)

Mesilas Yesharim teaches that we are obligated to cleanse ourselves of all aspects of anger by means of diligent study of this subject, regular introspection, and avoiding levity, scoffers, and other negative associations.

(We suggest also that you read our book *Guard Your Anger* [Southfield: Targum/Feldheim, 1999].)

Chapter Thirteen

Benefits of Laughter

Hashem has given us a wonderful gift — the gift of laughter. When utilized properly, laughter can greatly enhance our interpersonal relationships and our general sense of well-being.

Rav Shlomo Wolbe in *Alei Shur* teaches that a person should not be *makpid* (exacting) in his dealings with other people. Rather, it is important to train oneself to be easygoing and forgiving. How do we do this? Through developing a sense of humor.

Rav Wolbe explains that one who has a sense of humor will not become upset when people wrong him, for numerous reasons. He has compassion for the unfortunate, he forgives the weak-minded, he does not hold other people's weaknesses against them, he can rise above difficult situations, he sees light even in the midst of the negative, and he is always optimistic and forgiving.

The big question is how can a person train himself to develop a sense of humor? Rav Wolbe states that it is attainable through learning *mussar* properly! But the first step is to understand what is appropriate humor. Then one can find situations and opportunities for using humor.

Humor will enhance our lives immensely both internally and externally — it enables a person to be at peace with himself and to get along with others.

Laughter has the power to heal both the body and the soul. Many problems can be minimized if you joke about them and make them appear ridiculous. You can diffuse anxiety by exaggerating the situation to the point of absurdity. Laughing at problems helps to diminish their impact.

Many an argument between husband and wife has ended happily when one spouse says something humorous and causes both to burst into laughter. This laughing reprieve provides the couple with time to relax, change their thinking patterns, and patch up their difficulty.

We can learn to deal effectively with painful trials by utilizing humor, creativity, and trust in Hashem. "Humor" can be defined as developing the Torah perspective of the world. Focus on reality — Hashem is in complete control and He knows what is best for you! With this outlook, we will live long, healthy, and happy years.

Chapter Fourteen

Healthy Silence

I have found nothing better for the body than silence.

(*Avos* 1:17)

This *mishnah* teaches that the best way to protect one's health is to practice silence. Besides the mental and spiritual benefits gained from silence, which we learn from "Silence is a fence for wisdom" (ibid. 3:17) and "Anyone who speaks excessively comes to sin" (ibid. 1:17), we see here that silence can provide powerful physical benefits.

A person who learns the art of keeping silent will gain much in the area of physical health. Silence will save us from chest pain, headaches, sore throats, ulcers, stomach upsets, nervous tension, and even punches in the nose! It also relaxes our body, prevents anger and quarrels, and helps heal the body from many ailments.

The famous verse in *Tehillim* teaches, "Who is the person who desires life, who loves days to see good? Guard your tongue from evil and your lips from speaking deceit" (*Tehillim* 34:13–14). Refraining from speaking *lashon hara*, which includes focusing on silence, is one of the most potent methods for achieving a long life!

Silence is praise to Hashem.

(*Tehillim* 65:2)

The Gemara explains, based on this verse, that we cannot praise Hashem adequately because we know little about His infinite greatness (*Megillah* 18a). Thus, it is better to say to Hashem, "You are the Greatest, but who am I to do justice to You by voicing Your praises?" Showing that we are unable to say much is, in itself, the greatest praise.

Based on this, the *gemara* says that the best medicine is silence. How does the fact that silence is a form of praise to Hashem teach us that silence is the best medicine?

The most precious words in the world are words of praise to Hashem. There is nothing which will grant us a greater reward than reciting Hashem's praises. "It is good to give thanks to Hashem" (*Tehillim* 92:2). The greatest occupation, and the greatest of mitzvos, is to praise Hashem. However, silence is a greater form of praise. To say to Hashem, "I cannot praise You, for You are too great. I am speechless," is a greater expression of endearment than words of praise.

When a person praises Hashem with words, he might become arrogant and think that he has the ability to define the greatness of Hashem. By being silent, one is performing an even greater mitzvah, that of admitting the truth: Hashem is so infinitely supreme that we do not even know where to start in praising Him.

Let us imagine that for each word of praise to Hashem, one would be rewarded with a billion dollars. Even so, silence is still better. Thus, we can also deduce that in every other aspect of our lives, including our health, silence is the most beneficial method of gaining success. Silence is truly the greatest of all medicines.

Years ago, a man drowned in a bungalow colony pool. People were standing nearby as the man began to scream, "Help, I'm drowning!" but they ignored him. They were talking relaxedly, and the unfortunate fellow died.

How could such a thing happen? We would imagine that those people were completely wicked!

They were in the immediate vicinity and could have helped. A man is suddenly seized with cramps in the middle of a pool, and no one even attempts to save him?

Why did they ignore him?

The reason, it was discovered, was that the fellow was a well-known prankster. He was constantly joking and saying things which were not true, playing games, and fooling around. So when he began to shout for help, everyone automatically concluded that it was another one of his pranks. If one is always joking, how can it be discerned when he is finally telling the truth?

"I have found nothing better for the body than silence." If this person had practiced silence to an appropriate degree, he most likely would not have drowned.

This incident is similar to the story of the boy who cried "wolf." Eventually no one in town responded to his false cries because he was such a troublemaker. Subsequently, when a wolf did appear and he cried "wolf" in real alarm, no one came to his rescue and he was killed.

Life and death are in the power of the tongue.

(*Mishlei* 18:21)

Saying the wrong words at the wrong time can cause one's death. "I have found nothing better for the body than silence" can be applied literally to this episode.

Chapter Fifteen

The Rambam's Rules

The Rambam's guide to good health, as enumerated in *Hilchos Dei'os* 4:1–20, is as follows:

> Having a healthy and wholesome body is a primary service to Hashem, for it is impossible to fathom or to understand Torah knowledge when one is ill. Therefore, one must distance himself from that which harms the body and accustom himself to that which heals and maintains health.
>
> ❖ One should not eat unless he is hungry, nor drink unless he is thirsty.
>
> ❖ One should not restrain himself from moving his bowels.... Rather, one should take care of these needs immediately.

This point is based on the Talmudic teaching that one who delays a visit to the bathroom may transgress the prohibition of "You shall not make yourselves disgusting" (*Vayikra* 20:25). See *Shulchan Aruch, Orach Chaim* 3:17, where this halachah is stated explicitly.

❖ A person should not eat to fill his stomach entirely....

This concept is taught in the Gemara (*Gittin* 70a) in three variations: "One who eats to his capacity will become ill.... Eliyahu [the Prophet] taught: Eat a third, drink a third, and leave a third of your stomach empty.... One should refrain from eating before his stomach becomes full."

❖ One should not drink too much during a meal....

❖ One should not eat until he first attends to his bodily needs, if necessary (see *Shabbos* 41a).

❖ One should not eat until he has walked, until working up a sweat, worked, or otherwise exercised his body... (see *Sefer Shaarei Orah* 2:193).

❖ One should always sit while eating....

This is based on the Gemara, "There are three things that weaken one's strength: eating while standing or drinking while standing...." (*Gittin* 70a).

❖ One should not exert himself or exercise immediately after a meal.

❖ The day and night is twenty-four hours. It is sufficient for an individual to sleep one-third of this, which is eight hours...rising before sunrise.

❖ One should not sleep on his face or on his back, only on his side. [It is best] to start sleeping on the left side and finish on the right side.

❖ One should not sleep soon after eating. Rather, he should wait three or four hours after eating. One should not sleep during the daytime.

❖ One should eat foods that loosen the digestive system before eating a meal.

❖ If one wants to eat fowl and meat together, he should eat fowl first. One should always eat lighter food before heavy food.

❖ In the summer, one should eat cooler foods without many spices and use vinegar. In the winter, one should eat warm foods with spices and a little mustard. This system should also be applied to cold and warm climates.

❖ There are some foods that are harmful and should always be avoided: salted, aged, large fish; aged, salted cheese; mushrooms; old salted meat...and any food that has a foul odor or a very bitter taste. These may be as deadly poison to the body.

❖ There are other foods that are not as bad, [including]...large fish, beans, cabbage, and spices.... One should only eat small amounts of them infrequently. It also depends on the season.

❖ There are foods that are less harmful...but it is still not wise to eat these excessively. One who is wise and in control of his inclination and is not drawn after his desires will refrain from eating them entirely, unless he needs them for medical reasons.

❖ One should not eat some fruits excessively. Unripe fruits are harmful.... Figs, grapes, and almonds are always good, whether fresh or dry.

❖ Honey and wine are unhealthy for children but beneficial for elderly people, especially in the winter. One should eat less in the summer than the amount he eats during the winter.

The Gemara also cautions us to avoid eating eggs, garlic, or onions that were peeled and leftout overnight, since they can bring great harm to a person (*Niddah* 17a). The Klausenberger Rebbe, *zt"l*, said that this may be one of the causes of certain serious ailments that afflict people nowadays.

❖ A person should always see that his bowel movements remain regular. This is a leading principle in maintaining good health: constipation leads to intestinal disorders.

❖ Another rule has been given in regard to health matters: A person who exerts himself physically, does not fill his stomach, and keeps his digestive system on the loose side will be healthy and strong....

❖ On the other hand, one who sits around idly and does not exert himself physically, or delays moving his bowels or is always constipated...will always suffer and lack strength.

❖ Overeating is like poison to all people and is a primary cause of illness. Most illnesses are caused either by eating harmful foods or by overeating even healthy foods. This is what Shlomo said in his wisdom, "One who guards his mouth [from eating unhealthy foods or overeating], and his tongue [from speaking unnecessarily] will be spared many troubles" (*Mishlei* 21:23).

❖ One should wash himself [at least] once in seven days. One should not bathe immediately before eating, nor when he is hungry. After using hot water, one should use warm water and then cold water... (see *Shabbos* 41a).

❖ One should check whether he needs to relieve himself before and after a bath, before and after a meal, before and after intimate relations, before and after exercise, before and after sleep.

❖ One should be careful to dress warmly after a bath...and rest a bit.

❖ One should not overindulge in intimate relations.

Every person who maintains these practices is guaranteed not to be ill during his lifetime, until he becomes very old. He shall not need a physician and he will be healthy all his days, unless he was born with a defect, he conducted himself improperly, or there is an epidemic or famine.

Rav Eliyahu Lopian, *zt"l*, once refused a food that he was offered, saying, "I'm sorry, but my doctor doesn't allow me to eat that food." Some time later, he was asked which doctor he was referring to. He replied, "The Rambam."

Chapter Sixteen

Breakfast Benefits

Eating breakfast is beneficial for the whole body.

(*Gittin* 69b)

This advice should not be taken lightly. We see it repeated in several places in the Gemara, with emphasis on different benefits that we gain.

Rabbi Akiva instructed his son in seven different areas of behavior, one of which was "Rise early and eat breakfast in the summer [to protect yourself] from the sun and in the winter [to protect yourself] from the cold" (*Pesachim* 112a).

Another *gemara* informs us that "A person will be healthy, energetic, and spared from many illnesses by eating breakfast" (*Bava Kama* 92b).

It is important to eat a healthy breakfast, low on fat and sugar. We learn from the Gemara in *Bava Metzia* (107b) that a person will be spared from eighty-three different illnesses by eating some bread and drinking some water for breakfast. Furthermore, a person derives thirteen benefits from eating breakfast. They are:

1. The effects of the heat of the day are minimized.

2. The effects of cold are minimized.

3. The effects of wind are minimized.

4. One is protected from harmful forces.

5. One's wisdom is fortified.

6. One is able to defend himself and emerge victorious from confrontations (because his mind is more alert).

7. One has peace of mind for Torah study.

8. One has peace of mind for teaching Torah.

9. One is more likely to be listened to.

10. One's memory is improved.

11. One's body does not perspire.

12. One will be able to control his mind and avoid immoral thoughts.

13. Intestinal worms are killed.

Some Sages add that eating breakfast prevents jealousy and anger, as well as promoting patience and good will.

Chapter Seventeen

Changing Our Signals

Many health problems today are the result of overeating. When we indulge in too much food, we burden our stomachs, livers, kidneys, intestines, and eliminative organs. In addition, people who are overweight are more likely to contract fatal diseases and suffer from heart attacks.

It is important to learn to enjoy the quality of the food we eat, not the quantity. By eating less and exercising more, we can improve our health and our lives.

The Mishnah in *Avos* (2:8) teaches us an important lesson:

Marbeh basar — The more one increases [his] flesh [by overeating], *marbeh rimah* — the more he increases the worms [which will devour his flesh in the grave].

Because this is a disturbing image, it will help

us to control our eating habits. Train your mind to equate overeating with attracting worms. Repeat the Mishnah's words over and over to yourself until they become part of you. Would you eat a second piece of cake if you realized how much harm it could cause?

Rabbeinu Yonah on this *mishnah* explains the underlying message in it. People think they are enhancing their lives by indulging in more physical pleasures. However, if they would realize that this behavior will not only fail to enhance their lives, but will actually increase their suffering, they would act differently. The Bartenura writes that the pain worms inflict on the deceased is similar to the feeling of needles being stuck into a living person.

When we focus on these Torah thoughts, it will be easier for us to control our behavior.

Abarbanel explains the above *mishnah* in the following manner: There are people whose ambition in life is enjoy themselves by eating and drinking, thinking that this will maintain their health and prolong their lives. However, the *mishnah* teaches that they are falling into a trap they are digging themselves. Excessive eating only hastens a person's death, and the worms will have more to eat!

Abarbanel then lists a number of thoughts that will help motivate us to eat in moderation:

1. One who indulges in excessive eating will get a bad reputation. People will think less of him.

2. Excessive eating doesn't enhance the essence of a person (the mind or soul), only the superficial self, the body. Your body is not the real you! It is merely the vehicle for your great soul.

3. The results of overeating will not benefit a person after death. You cannot take it with you.

4. Excessive eating alienates one from Torah and Torah ideals.

5. Overeating does not increase one's *Olam HaZeh* or his *Olam HaBa*.

Our bodies are the most important piece of equipment we own. We must fuel them properly by eating the right foods in the right amounts. If you are tempted to keep eating beyond what is healthy, ask yourself, *What can I do now to give myself pleasure instead of eating?*

The Mishnah (*Avos* 2:7) provides us with an answer:
The more Torah study, the more life.

The more you eat, the more worms will attack you, but the more you learn, the more life you will have. Remind yourself constantly, *I want life, not death!* Involve yourself more in Torah, prayer, and acts of kindness to enjoy life more in every way.

Chapter Eighteen

Gaining Control

Rabbeinu Yonah (in *Yesod HaTeshuvah*) quotes a fundamental teaching of Rav Avraham:

> The following system is a great and wonderful barrier to assist in controlling one's appetite. One should not refrain completely from eating because it suffices to follow the Torah's guidelines for a proper diet. However, when one has the desire to eat more, one should leave some of the food over in honor of his Creator! This approach will help to protect one from sin, and it will remind him to love Hashem, more than if he would fast once a week. This should be a daily practice: leave some of your desires unfulfilled for the sake of Hashem's honor.

This is an amazing approach which will help us achieve control of our lives in many ways.

Similarly, the Gra (on *Mishlei* 1:2) warns:

"When one endeavors to break his desires, he must follow the Torah approach and not begin breaking his desires by fasting all week...."

We will not be successful, in the long run, if we attempt to diminish our physical pleasures without replacing them with spiritual pleasures. Ask yourself, *Am I an animal that merely eats all day? Why should I ruin my body and health by eating senselessly all day?*

Instead of eating, enjoy life by increasing your Torah study, prayer, or *chesed* involvement. Tackle your eating problem by "turning the tables" away from food to positive substitutes.

The next time you have an urge to eat unnecessarily, try reviewing a chapter of *Tehillim* that has special meaning to you instead. Develop this *Tehillim* review as a substitute form of indulgence. Another option is to take a ten-minute walk or do an exercise routine, do someone a favor, pick up a *sefer* and learn for five minutes, or say a prayer. If you find it difficult to motivate yourself, use the phrase from the Mishnah — "The more flesh, the more worms" — as a trigger.

This mode of behavior may be difficult to implement at first, as all new mitzvah programs are. However, the more you use it, the more spiritual weight you will gain (which is never harmful!).

Train yourself to think, "More food means more worms." Repeat it to yourself ten times in the morning and ten times before you go to bed. Perhaps even apply this concept to a particular food that tempts you. Imagine that wonderful dish crawling with worms!

The trick to making this work when you need it is to practice it when you do not need it. Make the idea a part of you so that it can be utilized at times of temptation.

Pirkei Avos teaches this system with the use of the term "he used to say." The great sages would review certain principles over and over again so they would become automatic responses. We can do the same thing if we work at it.

Chapter Nineteen

Planning the Approach

Perhaps you have tried to diet many times but have only been partially successful. It is easy to become frustrated and give up, but the truth is that you can still succeed if you learn new methods of control.

Analyze the reasons that you've failed in the past. Then study Chazal's teachings regarding the ways to achieve success.

The Gemara teaches:

In the way one wishes to go, he is led.

(*Makkos* 10b)

We need willpower and determination in order to succeed. If one is determined to succeed and tries his best, Hashem will assist him in his efforts.

Learn the tricks to success. If a tempting food is in front of you and you keep telling yourself, "I'm not going to eat it," you will probably not be able to control yourself. The Sages warn us, "The eyes see, the heart desires, and then the person takes action [in this case, eating]" (*Rashi, Bemidbar* 15:39).

Remove the tempting food from sight and, if possible, from the house.

Mesilas Yesharim (ch. 15) explains: "The fact that the inclinations are so strongly attuned to these pleasures and that so much effort and strategy are needed to restrain them is due to the persuasion of the eyes. The eyes tempt us by the appearance of things that look good and pleasurable. This is the persuasion that caused the first sin to be committed, as the verse testifies: 'The woman saw that the tree was good to eat and that it was tempting to the eyes' (*Bereishis* 3:6)."

Don't leave the bag of potato chips on the table and think, *I will only eat one. Just one more and that will be it!* Instead of fooling yourself, get up and put the bag away or ask someone else to put it away — out of sight!

This leads us to another teaching of Chazal:

> A mitzvah leads to another mitzvah, while a transgression leads to another transgression.
>
> (*Avos* 4:2)

If you think, *I'll just take one small piece*, you'll find yourself taking another and another as a direct result of this principle.

In addition, we have to keep the principle of "*Tafasta mu'at tafasta* — If you grasp a small amount, you will succeed" (*Sukkah* 5a) in mind. Don't try to change all your eating habits all at once. Make small changes one at a time.

> A *person's foolishness causes him to fail, but he blames Hashem.*
>
> (*Mishlei* 19:3)

The Gra teaches that the foolishness referred to in this verse is ignoring one's personal level and attempting to jump too high at once. A person has to climb gradually, as one climbs up a ladder — rung by rung. If he does not do this, "he causes himself to fail." He was not afforded assistance from Heaven because his approach was improper.

Then "he blames Hashem." This foolish person feels that Hashem has betrayed him by not fulfilling His promise to provide assistance. However, the truth is that Hashem only promises to assist those who work sensibly to achieve, via an approach that is compatible with their personalities.

If you recognize your mistakes, you will be one step closer to correcting them and achieving your goals. The ideas set out here should help you to approach dieting properly and meet with success!

Chapter Twenty

Prayers for Healthy Eating

Before praying for Torah to penetrate into one's system, one should first pray that sweets do not enter his system.

(Tana D'Vei Eliyahu Rabba 26)

One who has a sweet tooth will have a more difficult time controlling his weight than other people. The solution is to work on developing a "sensible tooth," to eat the proper foods in limited amounts.

Filling oneself with unhealthy foods makes it difficult to eat healthy foods. If a person's system is conditioned to the intake of sweets and empty calories, he will be repulsed by healthy food. This principle applies spiritually as well. One who enjoys Torah and mitzvah pursuits will be satisfied in a meaning-

ful way and will thus refrain from overeating to satisfy himself or to occupy his time. The Gra (on
Mishlei 2:19) writes, "The desire for physical pleasures is the opposite of Torah," and then cites the
above *midrash*.

For this reason, we request in *Birkas HaTorah*,
"Please make the words of Your Torah sweet in our
mouths and in the mouths of Your people, Yisrael."
This blessing is in actuality a prayer that our
mouths should be conditioned to relish the
sweetness of Torah, and not conditioned to uncon-
trolled eating.

When we pray for health three times a day in
Shemoneh Esrei (in the blessing of *Refa'einu*), we are
also asking for assistance in maintaining our health
through proper eating habits. Similarly, when we
pray for longevity, we should consider our dietary
needs, since eating healthy foods will maintain and
promote our health and our lives.

In the next blessing of *Shemoneh Esrei*, when we
pray for prosperity, we say, "And satiate us from
Your goodness." The Gra, in *Avnei Eliyahu*, explains
this request in two ways:

1. The food we eat should be blessed in our bodies,
   as we conclude in the prayer for rain at the end
   of Sukkos and in the prayer for dew on the first

day of Pesach: "For satiation, not for unrequited hunger."

2. We should be satiated and satisfied with even part of Hashem's goodness, so that we do not indulge ourselves more than necessary.

Chapter Twenty-one

Eating According to Halachah

It is helpful to periodically review the halachos of eating properly.

Rambam states emphatically:

"Overeating is like poison to all people and it is a primary cause of illness. Most illnesses are caused either by eating harmful foods or by overeating even healthy foods"

(*Hilchos De'os* 4:15).

This is the meaning of Shlomo HaMelech's teaching: "One who guards his mouth and tongue saves his soul from troubles" (*Mishlei* 21:23). It is essential to guard one's mouth from eating unhealthy foods and from overeating.

One of the first commandments given to mankind involved food: "From the Tree of Knowledge of Good and Bad, do not eat from it" (*Bereishis* 2:17). We see that food temptations have been influencing mankind since the very beginning of history. Perhaps because of this Hashem has given us so many commandments regarding food. Most of our daily domestic halachah concerns revolve around food, to remind us that even though we must eat to care for our bodies like the rest of mankind, we are still a holy, special nation.

A Jew is commanded to refrain from eating non-kosher types of fish, fowl, insects, and animals; kosher animals with blemishes, kosher animals which were improperly slaughtered or prepared; mixtures of meat and dairy products; produce from Israel from which the proper tithes and separations were not yet taken; *chametz* on Pesach; and all food and drink on fast days.

Before eating anything, we not only have to deal with the issue of basic kashrus and preparation, but also with the proper blessings for the food.

The Gemara (*Berachos* 35a) teaches, "The world and all it contains belongs to Hashem" (*Tehillim* 24:1). Hashem only permits man to partake of His property when we make a blessing first, acknowledging Hashem's kindness, wisdom, and mastery. When a person recites a blessing, Hashem consents to the verse, "He gave the earth to man" (ibid. 115:16).

As Jews, we should eat *l'sheim Shamayim*, for the sake of Heaven (*Avos* 2:17 and *Shulchan Aruch, Orach Chaim* 231).

We should share our food with others who are needy. In addition, we must eat the proper amount: neither too little, for we are obligated to provide and care for our bodies, nor too much, since this is also harmful. We need to focus on these guidelines daily in order to fulfill the general obligation to guard one's health and safety (*Devarim* 4:9).

Chapter Twenty-two

Utilizing Food

When Yitzchak Avinu wanted to bless his son Eisav, he called him and instructed him to prepare some tasty food, "so that my soul will bless you before I die" (*Bereishis* 27:4).

There is an amazing lesson contained in this brief episode. Our father Yitzchak considered it proper and essential to prepare himself by eating before he blessed his son, so that his blessing would be more sincere and heartfelt. The vehicle he used for the blessing was having Eisav prepare and serve his favorite food.

In the same way, we can understand the only blessing that is explicitly required by the Torah, the obligation to recite Birkas HaMazon after eating. "You shall eat and be satiated, and you shall bless Hashem, your God" (*Devarim* 8:10). When we eat, we should be thinking of Hashem's great kindness in supplying us with delicious food. This awareness inspires us to bless Hashem.

> *Persuasion is only by food and drink.*
>
> (Chullin 4b)

This principle teaches us that when we eat and drink we are to be motivated to serve Hashem more enthusiastically. This begins with reciting blessings properly before and after we eat.

It is important to apply Rambam's teaching:

> *One should not eat all that he desires as a dog or a donkey does, but, rather, he should eat those foods that are beneficial to the body, whether they are bitter or sweet.*
>
> (Dei'os 3:2)

However, when there is a choice of two beneficial foods, one of which is tastier than the other, it's appropriate to choose the one you like better, for two reasons: First, a tasty food will arouse a more successful digestive response, and second, it will evoke from you a deeper sense of gratitude to Hashem (Rabbi Avigdor Miller, *The Beginning*, p. 423).

Food has the potential of serving as a powerful motivator in one's service of Hashem. However, it can also be a potential stumbling block that the evil inclination uses, as the Gra stresses (on *Mishei* 7:14):

The yetzer hara will not entice a person to commit an obvious sin, for he will surely refuse. Instead, it will find opportunities to entice the individual in regard to food-related mitzvos. Thus, we must be very, very careful not to be misled.

Just as the first sin in world history was caused by enticing fruits (*Bereishis* 3:6), so too, Eisav lost his birthright as the result of a passion for food.

The Torah recounts that Eisav told Yaakov:

Please give me to eat of that red-red, because I am weary....

(Bereishis 25:30)

Eisav did not specify "food." Rather, he referred to the color of the dish that he saw. He followed the desire of his eyes, repeating the word *red*.

The word *haliteini*, "give me to eat," is a coarse expression used in the Gemara for the process of stuffing livestock before slaughter. Eisav requested food with an animalistic passion, like animals which follow their eyes to satisfy their physical urges. A person who lives solely to gratify his bodily needs is behaving like an animal.

Eisav's desire for the food Yaakov was cooking led him to sell his birthright, losing the opportunity to excel in the service of Hashem. His attitude is typified by the wicked who say:

Eat and drink, for tomorrow we shall die....

(*Yeshayah* 22:13)

We learn from Eisav, who was a progenitor of the nations of the world, how following the eyes and physical lusts leads one away from the Torah and its fulfillment.

The Gra teaches us that our physical desires should be channeled and kept under control for the service of Hashem. In order to do this, we must properly care for our bodies. The goal is to subdue and control them, not destroy them.

A desire that is broken [nihiyah] is a sweetness to the soul.

(*Mishlei* 13:19)

The Gra explains that although controlling one's desires is initially painful, it will eventually lead to great pleasure and satisfaction for the soul. In addition, the Gra explains that the word *nihiyah* also means "fulfilled." Thus, "a fulfilled desire," which is a broken desire, leaves one spiritually fulfilled.

The idea behind this concept is that when one forgoes his desires for Hashem's honor, he is rewarded measure-for-measure — Hashem will fulfill his desires. The Mishnah (*Avos* 2:4) teaches: "If you fulfill Hashem's desires as if they were your own, Hashem will fulfill your desires as if they were His own." Thus, by controlling your desires you will ultimately be achieving them.

The evil inclination tries to assure a person that indulgences will do him good. To oppose this, Shlomo HaMelech teaches:

> *A tooth that is ro'ah and a foot that slips are caused by the guarantee of a traitor on the day of trouble.*
> (*Mishlei* 25:19)

The word *ro'ah* has two meanings: "well fed" and "harmful" (*Gra*). Thus, the verse is explained as follows: one who heeds the false guarantees of his traitorous "friend" (the evil inclination) that he can keep eating as much as he pleases will suffer broken teeth (i.e., his teeth will eventually decay and he will be unable to eat).

Chapter Twenty-three

Health Choices

We all have a choice every day as to how we fuel our body, the gift that Hashem granted us. Making the right choices can make all the difference in our lives. If we fail to eat properly or exercise properly, we must face the consequences.

The Rambam emphasizes, "Overeating is like death to all people and a primary cause of illness" (*Hilchos Dei'os*). It is estimated that hundreds of thousands of people die prematurely each year because of lack of poor diets and insufficient physical activity.

Doctors tell us that many common illnesses are caused or aggravated by overeating, including heart disease, stroke, cancer, and diabetes. Why allow this to happen to you? Do not take your health for granted — you must think about your body's needs daily in order to minimize health risks.

The Gemara teaches, "Carrying loads and exercising is beneficial for it warms up the body" (*Gittin* 67b). The Rambam cites this lesson in *Hilchos Dei'os*, when he writes that people should exercise every morning before breakfast.

If you find it difficult to maintain a regular exercise routine, you can still find opportunities to exercise throughout the day. For example:

❖ Use the stairs instead of the elevator for three or four flights.

❖ Don't park directly in front of a store. Leave that spot for others; park a block or two away instead.

❖ Take a walk during your lunch break.

I thank You, Hashem, for the awesome wonders You made me with....

(*Tehillim* 139:14)

When we learn about and focus on the complex and wondrous body we were given, we will be more motivated to care for it properly.

It is estimated that the human brain can store about 280 quintillion bits of memory. It's an amazing system! Yet when we overeat or fail to get enough sleep, we are undermining our health and reducing our mental clarity. Our bodies are holy vessels that we must take care of. Do not make light of your own health.

Would you willingly increase your risk of heart attack, lung cancer, and stroke? Would you smoke nicotine if you knew it would make you look and feel old before your time? Look at X-rays of diseased lungs which have become that way through smoking. Look at pictures of clogged arteries which are the result of overeating. This will help you control your bad habits which can ruin your health.

> *A small amount of salt is healthy; too much is harmful.*
>
> (*Berachos* 34a)

This is an important lesson to keep in mind. Some people, out of habit, liberally salt their food before they even taste it. Salt is essential for one's health, since it helps regulate the body's fluids and blood pressure. But overdoing it can be harmful. We need to train ourselves to remember this *gemara* at mealtimes to avoid using too much salt.

Would you teach others to care for their health the way you care for yours? If that question makes you pause, perhaps it is time to rethink your habits and find new patterns for eating, sleeping, and exercising. You owe it to yourself!

Conclusion

Hashem gave us the Torah to help us reach perfection. To achieve this goal, we must use what we were given to develop and maintain our health and to release our potential spiritual greatness.

The key to change is to envision the future you. If you need to exercise more, improve your eating habits, or change your attitude toward safety, picture your life in detail once you have achieved your goal. You will find it much easier to make strides toward improvement with this picture in mind. "A wise person anticipates the future" (*Tamid* 32a).

If you want to constantly be in a good mood, you must live a healthy, balanced lifestyle. Get adequate sleep, eat balanced meals, take walks, and exercise. There's no other way to pursue your goal of perfection.

Health and safety go hand in hand. Besides following a good eating plan and exercising regularly, we must keep in mind the Torah's command to "guard your life exceedingly." If we don't take the proper precautions, making sure our houses are safe and our environments are danger-free, we will find ourselves transgressing the Torah's laws and risking our lives without even realizing it. Our safety and the safety of those around us is a number-one priority.

This work merely touches on the Torah topics that need to be researched and worked on intensely for a person to succeed in living a productive, spiritual life. In addition, the following pages, safety guidelines from Hatzalah, must be incorporated into our daily lives. With these we will be able to achieve our maximum potential and grow in Torah.

When a person does his part in caring for his health and safety, Hashem helps him succeed in his endeavors.

Safety Guidelines

Reprinted with permission of
Hatzalah

How to Prevent Fires and Burns

1. Consult your *rav* concerning where to place Shabbos and *yom tov* candles when young children will be present.

2. Do not leave pot handles extending over the stove. Turn them inward, away from neighboring flames.

3. Do not cook with a flame that extends beyond the pot bottom.

4. Do not wear loose sleeves or plastic aprons when cooking — no loose clothing that can hang over the flame. Tie back long hair when cooking.

5. Do not congregate in the kitchen! Children should not be in the kitchen when the oven is being used or hot foods are being transferred.

6. Never place hot liquids or foods near the table or counter edge.

7. Always use a protecting plate or saucer underneath hot liquids. Do not just carry the bowl or pot.

8. Never serve or pass anything over a child — or anyone.

9. Do not serve hot food or drinks to children until they have cooled sufficiently to be eaten directly.

10. Never, never leave children unattended with candles (Shabbos, Chanukah, etc.).

11. Make sure that your children cannot climb up a chair or stool near a gas range.

12. Do not turn on the hot water faucet first when washing or showering. First turn on the cold, then adjust with the hot water.

13. Check electric cords and plugs and cover open sockets.

14. Buy and install smoke detectors.

15. Keep flammable materials away from the home heating system and hot water units.

16. Cover radiators and keep children away from portable room heaters.

17. Do not iron clothes when young children are around. Never leave a hot iron alone in a room with children around.

18. Never place an aerosol can near heat or flame. They can explode!

19. Always place glass *yartzeit* candles on a metal tray. They can burst and cause a fire.

20. Consult your *rav* on how to search for *chametz* safely. Burning *chametz* should always be done by adults, not children.

Fire Safety

1. Window safety guards must open easily and quickly by an adult or older child.

2. If, *chas v'shalom*, you are on fire, don't run. Stop, drop, and roll on the ground quickly.

3. Think and plan ahead. Develop a family escape plan.

4. Use night-lights in every strategic place in the house.

5. If, *chas v'shalom*, a major fire breaks out, evacuate immediately! Do not stop for anything and do not reenter.

The best place for your smoke detectors:

❖ outside the bedrooms

❖ on each level in the home

Take care of them:

❖ test monthly

❖ replace battery once a year or when they make
a chirping sound

Home Safety

1. Buy and install smoke detectors.
2. Buy and install safety window bars.
3. Keep stairways free of objects.
4. Keep a list of emergency numbers by all phones.
5. Make sure your address is in large, clearly visible letters on your house.

Young children can strangle in the loop of pull cords, chain and bead cords, and cords that run through window coverings. They can also wrap cords around their necks. To avoid strangulation and entanglement, keep cords out of reach of young children. Also:

1. Install safety devices that remove the cord loop or reduce access to cords.
2. Move cribs and furniture away from window coverings.

Baby-at-Home Safety Checklist

1. Knot blind and curtain cords every four inches and place out of reach.

2. Secure baby from falling when changing diaper.

3. Keep baby powder and all other supplies away from the baby's reach.

4. Toy boxes should have ventilation holes and light lids. (No lid is best.)

5. Guard the baby from all small objects: pins, toy parts, rubber bands, balloons, etc.

6. Keep hair dryer and other appliances unplugged and put away.

7. Set hot water at 120 degrees or less. Turn on cold water first. Test water before bathing baby.

8. Empty bathtub, and all water containers, immediately after use.

Choking Prevention for Infants and Children

1. Do not feed children younger than four years old any round, firm foods unless they're chopped completely. These types of foods are common choking dangers. Infants and young children often don't chew their food well, so they sometimes attempt to swallow it whole.

   Common choking dangers for infants and children include: hot dogs, nuts, chunks of meat, grapes, hard candy, popcorn, chunks of peanut butter, raisins, raw carrots, balloons, coins, marbles, small toy parts, pen caps, and small button-type batteries.

2. Insist that children eat while sitting at the table; children should never walk, run, or play with food in their mouths.

3. Prepare and cut food for young children and teach them to chew their food well.

4. Supervise mealtimes for young children. Many choking cases occur when older brothers or sisters offer unsafe foods to a younger child.

5. Avoid toys with small parts and keep other small household items out of reach of young children.

Check It Out!

If your child is choking, use the following as a guide:

1. Find out if the child can breathe, cry, or speak. See if the child has a strong cough. (A strong cough means there is little or no blockage and the child may dislodge the item if there is a blockage.)

2. Do not start first aid if there is a strong cough or if there is little or no blockage. This can turn a partial blockage into a complete blockage. If the child is coughing, crying, or speaking, call your doctor for further advice.

Safety Facts for Babies

1. Sleeping: The American Academy of Pediatrics (AAP) has made a recommendation for infants to be placed on their sides or on their backs rather than on their stomachs for the first four to six months of their lives. These guidelines are based on research from Australia and New Zealand which showed a substantial reduction in the occurrence of sudden infant death syndrome (SIDS) when babies sleep on their backs. The problem seems to be that infants that lack proper muscle control may linger in face-into-the-mattress position and may suffocate, *chas v'shalom*.

2. Vitamins: Even a small amount of iron in multiple vitamins could be poisonous for a child if it exceeds the dosage. Therefore, treat these multiple vitamins as you would any other potentially

hazardous medication — keep them far out of the reach of children. Safety caps are not foolproof, and there have been occasions when even two-year-olds have successfully disengaged a childproof cap.

3. Walkers: In 1993, twenty-five thousand children were injured by baby walkers. One-fourth of the injuries were described as severe (fractures and head injuries) and most were caused by falls involving stairs. Walkers increase a baby's height and give him mobility and access to areas that may be extremely dangerous. The AAP has attempted to have them banned, but the industry is resistant. Exercise extreme caution if you must use them.

4. Balloons and streamers: The U.S. Consumer Product Safety Commission (CPSC) warns that children can strangle if they become entangled in ribbons or streamers hanging from wall decorations near the crib or within reach of children. CPSC knows of one death and one injury to young children who became entangled in the ribbons of wall decorations which were hung near cribs. Parents should keep wall decorations with ribbons or streamers away from cribs and

well away from where children play to prevent entanglement and strangulation.

5. Crib toys: Crib gyms, exercisers, kickers, and similar toys are attractive additions to a child's environment, but they are dangerous as well. The risk of strangulation begins when children are just starting to push up on hands and knees, usually about five months old. Children can pull themselves up to a hanging crib toy and become entangled or fall forward over it, but they cannot disentangle themselves, support their own weight, or lift themselves off the toy. The results can be injury or death.

   Completely remove such toys from the crib or playpen. Do not merely untie one end and allow the toy to dangle because strangulation is still a possibility.

6. Cribs: Cribs also pose a hazard for newborns and infants. Any crib manufactured before 1974 may pose a strangulation hazard. The vertical slats of a crib should be no more than 2 3/8" apart. Make sure that there are no missing or cracked bars or slats, and that no decorative cutouts on the crib ends are large enough to trap a baby's head. Check screws and bolts: they

should be tightly fitted. The mattress should fit snugly within the crib, with no gaps that may trap a baby's head.

7. Strollers: The CPSC warns that babies can die if they are left unattended while sleeping in strollers. They may slip feet-first through a leg opening and become entrapped by the head between the seat and the hand-rest bar. Since 1986, eight infant entrapment deaths and two nonfatal incidents have been reported. In each of the incidents, the infants had been left to sleep in a stroller with the backrest in the flat, carriage position. To avoid incidents of entrapment in stroller leg openings, CPSC advises infant caretakers to:

❖ Never leave a child unattended in a stroller. This is especially important if the stroller seat's backrest is down.

❖ Be aware that infants only a few weeks old can creep or move when asleep. The youngest victim was an infant just seven weeks old.

8. Shopping carts: Falls from shopping carts are among the leading causes of head injuries to young children treated in hospital emergency rooms. The CPSC estimated that in 1988 there

were twelve thousand hospital emergency room treated head injuries to children under five years of age. These injuries were usually due to falls from shopping carts. About one-third of these head injuries were concussions, fractures, or internal injuries.

Shopping carts are now often used in hardware stores, drugstores, toy stores, and grocery stores. To prevent falls, use seat belts to restrain the child in the cart and watch the child closely while shopping.

Toddler-at-Home Safety Checklist

1. Make sure that your child is never underfoot when you are cooking, transferring hot liquids, or ironing clothes.

2. Be sure that the surface under play equipment is of material soft enough to absorb a fall without causing an injury.

3. Use gates on stairways and install window guards in all windows.

4. When crossing the street with your child, use the opportunity to teach him or her to cross safely: look left and right and then left and right again.

5. Always walk behind your car to see that no children are there before you back out of a driveway.

6. Do not leave a chair next to a kitchen counter, oven, or range.

7. Never leave your toddler alone in a bathtub, in a wading or swimming pool, near a pail of water, or near any water, even for a moment.

8. Use a car safety seat *every time* your toddler rides in a car.

Toy Safety

1. Not all toys are for all kids; toys must be specifically selected for each child.

2. Look for and follow label instructions on all toys.

3. Beware of toys with sharp edges and points, small parts, cords, and strings.

4. Do not buy toys which make noise loud enough to damage hearing.

5. Flying toys such as arrows and darts can become weapons and cause serious eye injuries.

6. Children should be taught to use electric toys properly and only under adult supervision.

7. Infant toys, such as rattles, teethers, and squeeze toys, should be large enough that they cannot become lodged in the child's throat, and should be easily removable from the mouth.

Many children have choked on rattles that were too small! Make sure that it is impossible for your baby to ever choke on his rattle.

8. Remove all crib toys that are strung across the crib or playpen when your baby begins to push up on his hands.

Erev Shabbos Alerts

1. Consult a *rav* concerning where to light Shabbos candles when young children are present.

2. Never leave children unattended with burning candles.

3. After lighting candles have someone place matches securely away.

4. Place the spout of a hot water urn away from counter edge. Do not use an extension cord or leave it within child's reach.

5. Children should not be in the kitchen while preparations for Shabbos are being made.

6. Start Shabbos preparations early. Last-minute rushing causes hazardous and hectic situations.

7. Never hold a child while drinking a hot liquid.

8. Take all phones off the hook before bathing children.

9. Have all necessary equipment with you before putting your child in a bath.

10. Never, under any circumstances, leave a child alone in the tub — not even for a moment! Take the child with you!

Poison Prevention

Facts

1. Death from disease is declining, while death from household poisonings are rising.

2. Three thousand people die annually from poisoning by regular household products.

3. Two hundred children die annually. Two hundred and fifty thousand are saved due to medical attention received in time, but some of the injuries can last a lifetime.

Lock Up, High Up

Your greatest defense against poisoning in the home is to place all poisonous substances in the high cabinets in the kitchen, bathroom, workroom, and bedroom. Rather than put cleaning substances under the sink, place paper goods and nontoxic items there. Place all toxic items and cleaners in a high cabinet out of chair and stool reach — and out of sight. Do the same for all medicines and ointments kept in the bathroom and solutions used in the workroom.

What to Watch Out For

1. Kitchen: detergents, drain cleaners, scouring powder, oven cleaner, furniture polish, floor wax, metal polish, wax remover, wall cleaner, ammonia, floor cleaner, pure food extracts (some are poisonous if not diluted), steel wool cleaning pads.

2. Bathroom: aspirin, prescription drugs, rubbing alcohol, liniment, laxatives, tinctures, boric acid. Do not let the toilet be a platform to reach cabinets — lock them up if necessary. Rinse out empty containers and flush away remaining and unused contents. Do not just rely on a childproof cap with your child's life.

3. Bedroom: hair spray, cologne, nail polish, polish remover, face cream, astringent.

4. Utility areas: solvents, turpentine, paint, varnish, paint thinner, pesticides, herbicides, auto waxes, polishes, dyes, charcoal starters, drain

opener, lye, glue, rat and ant poisons, gasoline, kerosene, bleach.

If your children are already grown, think about your grandchildren or the children of your relatives and friends. Your responsibility is greater than you realize.

Keep a bottle of syrup of ipecac (to induce vomiting) on the top shelf of the medicine cabinet and have the number of your poison control center handy, but don't depend on them.

Kid Safety

At Home

1. Never open the door for anyone without permission from your parents.

2. If the phone rings never say you are alone or "no one is home."

3. Always know where you can call for help in an emergency.

4. Do not leave the house without specific permission from your parents.

On the Phone

Children who are at home alone should know how to make phone calls, how to use the telephone in an emergency, and also how to politely answer telephone calls without revealing that they are alone. To insure their safety, children should not give any personal information to callers they don't know. Almost all calls can be handled by a child with the following three phrases:

1. "Who is this?"

2. "My mother/father is busy."

3. "Please call later."

School Bus Safety

1. Only cross the street in front of a bus — never in back of one.

2. Make sure that the driver can see you clearly.

3. At all times keep a safe distance from the bus.

4. When crossing in front of a bus, always come to a full stop at the other side of the bus and carefully look both ways for oncoming traffic.

5. Never stop to pick anything up when crossing a street.

Stranger Safety

1. Never go anywhere or accept a ride with any person unless your parents have specifically given you permission. If someone tries to force you to go somewhere with him, immediately leave and/or shout for help.

2. If a vehicle pulls up to you to ask directions, to request assistance in looking for a lost child or

pet, or for any other reason, stay at least a few feet away while answering. If you feel in any sort of danger, don't hesitate to tell the person that an adult will be able to assist him better and then quickly walk away, preferably toward people or stores.

3. Utilize a buddy system if at all possible when going places (school, home, outings, or out to play). The more buddies the better.

4. If anyone asks you to do anything that seems wrong or strange in any way, just say no and then tell your parents, teacher, or any other adult that you trust.

5. Don't wander around a public place by yourself. If you get separated from your family or friends, go to a security office, a checkout counter, or any other central, well-lit location and calmly, clearly, and loudly tell them the problem.

6. Tell your parents as soon as possible if someone touches you in a way that makes you feel uncomfortable or asks you to keep a "special secret."

7. Never hitchhike or accept a ride from someone unless your parents give you explicit permission to go.

Bicycle Safety

1. Wear a well-fitted helmet at all times.
2. Obey all traffic signs and lights.
3. Carefully look both ways before entering a street.
4. Watch for car doors opening.
5. Only one person at a time should ride on a bike.

Bike Safety Dress

1. Don't get caught up in a bike's chain: Always wear ankle clips, elastic bands, or tuck pants into socks.
2. Be visible: Wear bright-colored clothes by day and light-colored clothes at night.
3. Protect your head: Always wear an approved helmet.
4. Avoid slip-on shoes. They can easily fall off.

Bunk Bed Safety

1. Do not let young children sleep or play on the upper bunk.

2. Be sure there are guardrails on all sides of the bunk bed if it is not securely against the wall.

3. Rough play is unsafe around and on beds and other furniture.

4. Use a night-light so that children can see the ladder if they get up at night.

Babysitting Safety

Before you leave:

1. Give the sitter exact instructions for child care.

2. Tell the sitter which neighbor to call for assistance.

3. Leave number(s) where you can be reached at all times.

4. Give instructions for the alarm, thermostat, fuses, etc.

5. Give written instructions for special child care needs (medicine, allergies, and so on).

Driver Safety Test

1. Are you driving like a mensch, or are you endangering your life and the lives of others?
2. Are you a speed driver?
3. Do you signal when necessary?
4. Do you begin driving while the light is still red?
5. Do you and your passengers buckle up?
6. Is your vehicle in proper working condition?
7. Do you watch out for children playing in the street?

A Baby in the Car

1. Never leave children alone in the car.
2. Do not hold a child on your lap while traveling.
3. Every child must be firmly secured in a car seat.
4. Do not put a baby in the front seat, even in a baby seat.
5. Children must never be standing when the car is in motion.
6. Never leave your keys in the ignition when not driving.

Facts

1. If a baby is sitting on a lap in a car traveling thirty miles per hour and the driver hits the brakes, the baby will be crushed between the person holding him and the dashboard. This is the equivalent of dropping a baby from a third-

floor window. Use a safety seat for your infants!

2. Seat belts are not just for long trips — three-quarters of all traffic deaths occur within twenty-five miles of the victims' homes, at forty miles per hour or less.

3. Some people are thrown clear from accidents, unhurt. The chance of surviving a crash is five times as good if you stay inside the car.

Remember: buckling up everyone in the car takes less time than the ambulance ride to the hospital, the hospital stay, the regret, the therapy, and the tragedy that could last forever. Buckle up! As the driver of a car, you have the same authority as the captain of a plane or ship. Use your authority — buckle up and give the order for everyone else to follow.

(Facts supplied by General Motors)

Messages from Hatzalah

Hatzalah has less than four minutes to revive someone who has stopped breathing. Can you live with wasting three of them?

Case one: You're in shul on Shabbos or *yom tov* and someone collapses. Call Hatzalah, of course. But how? Perhaps you'll use phone in the *simchah* room downstairs...but it's locked. So you run to the phone in the hall, but who is carrying a quarter on Shabbos? And while you struggle to locate a phone, a life is quickly ending — a life that could have been saved.

It is imperative that each shul and *beis midrash* be equipped with an emergency phone that is directly connected to Hatzalah and located in a main area, accessible to all, for emergency use on

Shabbos, *yom tov*, and every day.

Case two: You run to the phone to call Hatzalah because a child is choking. You give Hatzalah your proper address and they assure you they're on their way. However, if you don't have house numbers prominently displayed on the outside of your home, your home can't be identified and precious moments that should be spent saving a life are wasted on finding an address (sometimes written on a garbage can).

Please be sure your address is properly displayed and clearly visible during the day and night. It can save your life, or the life of someone you love.

If You Ever Need to Call Hatzalah

- ❖ Speak slowly and clearly. If you are too nervous, have someone else speak.

- ❖ Make sure to give your phone number and address.

- ❖ Don't hang up until told to do so.

- ❖ Send an extra person outside to wait by the front door until Hatzalah arrives.

Hatzalah's Phone Numbers

New York: (718/212) 387-1750 or 230-1000

Lakewood: (732) 370-3600

Kiryas Yoel: (845) 783-1212

Kiryas Tosh: (450) 434-2222

Rockland County: (845) 425-1233

Montreal: (877) 341-1818

Toronto: (416) 780-9991